T0157120

KNOWLEDGE SHARING TUTORIAL

Where technology is advancing, economies challenged, and communities evolving, nothing is more essential than the development of learning resources in school and at work.

Dr. John Harrigan

iUniverse, Inc.
Bloomington

KNOWLEDGE SHARING TUTORIAL

iUniverse books may be ordered through booksellers or by contacting:

iUniverse
1663 Liberty Drive
Bloomington, IN 47403
www.iuniverse.com
1-800-Authors (1-800-288-4677)

Because of the dynamic nature of the Internet, any web addresses or links contained in this book may have changed since publication and may no longer be valid. The views expressed in this work are solely those of the author and do not necessarily reflect the views of the publisher, and the publisher hereby disclaims any responsibility for them.

Any people depicted in stock imagery provided by Thinkstock are models, and such images are being used for illustrative purposes only.

Certain stock imagery © Thinkstock.

ISBN: 978-1-4759-8558-0 (sc)
ISBN: 978-1-4759-8559-7 (e)

Library of Congress Control Number: 2013906678

Printed in the United States of America.

iUniverse rev. date: 04/15/2013

Knowledge
Sharing Tutorial

*Where technology is advancing,
economies challenged, and
communities evolving, nothing is
more essential than the development
of learning resources in school and at
work.*

Professor John E. Harrigan

Knowledge Sharing Tutorial Outline

Tutorial Overview

Part I. Knowledge Sharing Lessons

Lesson 1. Theory

Lesson 2. Method

Lesson 3. Process

Part II. Knowledge Sharing Studies

Study 1. Evolving School Learning Resources, Introducing New Thoughts and New Technology

Study 2. Building for the Future, A Promising Community Learning Center Opportunity

Study 3. Continuous Workforce Improvement, A Challenging Problem for Personalized Learning

Study 4. A Knowledge Sharing Research Strategy, Directed to Changing Social and Economic Conditions

Part III. Learn-by-Doing Assignments

1. Sign Into the Tutorial Web Site

2. Define the Evolving Learning Resource Study Objectives and Critical Success Factors

3. Develop Annotated Expert Knowledge References

4. Develop the Project Deliberation Agenda

5. Share Assignment Outcomes with Colleagues for Critique

Tutorial Overview

Where technology is advancing, economies challenged, and communities evolving, nothing is more essential than the development of learning resources in school and at work.

For this responsibility, when introducing new thoughts and new technology to promising opportunities, challenging problems, and changing conditions, the tutorial lessons and studies maintain the most effectively employable view on how to lead and manage evolving learning resources—learn from people and about people.

How do we learn from people and about people? Within the knowledge sharing method we use a rigorous process of questioning to identify promising learning resource possibilities and manage their development. A knowledge acquisition process that builds the pathway to evolving learning resource achievement; using information and communication technology to make learning resource project participants one deliberative body.

Spirit of Discovery

The core of the knowledge sharing process is a spirit of discovery—where in the scholarly traditions of critical thinking and thorough analysis we confirm the things we know, find out all we can about what we need to know, and decide what strategic research we need to assure that we discover the things we are unaware of but which may dramatically affect our learning resource development outcomes.

Maintain this spirit of discovery you gain recognition that

your leadership is well founded, assuring that once a learning resource project decision is made everyone understands it, able to move forward to an exceptional achievement.

To get the most out of the knowledge sharing tutorial think about the promising opportunities, challenging problems, or changing conditions in which you are engaged. How would application of the knowledge sharing theory, method, and process improve your leadership and achievements? Think about a future project: How will you lead and manage the introduction of new thoughts and new technology within your area of responsibility?

Evolving Learning Resources

To confirm the knowledge sharing tutorial as an essential learning experience, with appreciation for the thoughts provided, we take directly from a number of sources. Starting with *Towards Knowledge Societies*, published in 2005 by the United Nations Educational, Scientific and Cultural Organization. Where it is stated, "a knowledge society must foster knowledge sharing."

Towards Knowledge Societies provides these basic perspectives regarding the challenge of introducing new thoughts and new technology to education's promising opportunities, challenging problems, and changing conditions:

❖ Without critical judgment and thinking, as we analyze, sort and incorporate the items considered most interesting, information will never be anything but a mass of indistinct data. And instead of controlling it, many people will realize that it is controlling them.

❖ What is more, the tools that can be used to "process" that information are not always up to the task. In knowledge societies, everyone must be able to move easily through the flow of information submerging us, and to develop cognitive and critical thinking skills to distinguish between "useful" and "useless" information.

❖ We find support for the knowledge sharing tutorial emphasis on learning from people and about people, where *Towards Knowledge Societies* provides a knowledge sharing cultural view regarding the extent to which the introduction of new thoughts and new technology is accelerating change. A major international challenge when you consider every society has its own knowledge assets. It is therefore necessary to work towards connecting the forms of knowledge that societies already possess and the new forms of development, acquisition, and spread of knowledge.

The Asian Development Bank Report, *Enhancing Knowledge Management Under Strategy 2020: Plan of Action for 2009–2011*, confirms the knowledge sharing tutorial as an essential learning experience when you consider these thoughts: Despite worldwide attention to strategic planning, the notion of strategic practice is surprisingly new. To draw a strategy is relatively easy but to execute it is difficult—strategy is both a macro and a micro phenomenon that depends on synchronization. One should systematically review, evaluate, prioritize, sequence, manage, redirect, and if necessary even cancel strategic initiatives.

Confirming these views, the *Federal Ministry of Education and Research, Germany,* emphasizes that international competition for future opportunities has essentially become a competition for the quality of education systems, where education reform requires a national effort of all stakeholders and a broad debate in society across ideological barriers. There is a growing awareness that one-size-fits-all approaches to school knowledge and organization are ill adapted both to individuals' needs and to the knowledge society at large. To move beyond uniform, mass provision can be described as the "personalization" of education.

The U.S. Department of Education's 2010 plan, *Transforming American Education: Learning Powered by Technology,* similarly calls for a revolutionary transformation rather than evolutionary tinkering when developing community learning resource development. The plan urges learning resources that increase student engagement and motivation, using technology to transform teaching by ushering in a new model of connected teaching. This model links teachers to their students and to knowledge content, resources, and systems to help them improve the learning experience.

The following introduce the three parts of the knowledge sharing tutorial.

Part I. Knowledge Sharing Lessons

The knowledge sharing lessons establish questions as primary facts when introducing new thoughts and new technology to evolving learning resources. Questions have always guided the search for knowledge, particularly questioning to discover the exceptions that confound what has been accepted as true. Further, questions endure; it is the answers that vary.

The knowledge sharing lessons emphasize knowledge acquisition and essential information and communication technology (ICT) advantages, answering the following questions:

- ❖ How do we establish a means for individuals and groups to share experience and insights within evolving learning resources?
- ❖ How do we accumulate ideas and sharpen perceptions and at the same time assure rigorous analysis?
- ❖ How do we make knowledge acquisition processes repeatable, scalable, and executable across organizations?
- ❖ And, within all of this, how can we maintain the standard of complete, verified, applicable, and timely knowledge acquisition outcomes?

Part II. Knowledge Sharing Studies

Study 1. Evolving School Learning Resources, Introducing New Thoughts and New Technology

Study 2. Building for the Future, A Promising Community Learning Center Opportunity

Study 3. Continuous Workforce Improvement, A Challenging Problem for Personalized Learning

Study 4. A Knowledge Sharing Research Strategy, Directed to Changing Social and Economic Conditions

These studies are presented as learning experiences useful for school, university, corporate, business, institutional, and government entities, providing models for learning from people and about people and gaining the benefit of individual experience and insight.

The tutorial studies equate knowledge and shared responsibility with effective action, answering this question: How can we develop effective knowledge sharing experiences within evolving learning resources?

In the knowledge sharing experience the answer will be increasingly more positive as people recognize that the knowledge sharing process complements their expertise, experience, and insights—a means to achieve a dramatic improvement in opportunities for participants in a learning resource development project to exchange insights and points of view, and compare intentions and requirements.

Part III. Learn-by-Doing Assignments

From the perspective that writing is an intense learning experience, in the tutorial knowledge sharing assignments participants, individually or in groups, address a learning resource promising opportunity, challenging problem, or changing condition of interest. The outline for this work is:

1. Sign Into the Tutorial Web Site

2. Define the Evolving Learning Resource Study Objectives and Critical Success Factors

3. Develop Annotated Expert Knowledge References

4. Develop the Project Deliberation Agenda

5. Share Assignment Outcomes with Colleagues for Critique

Part I. Knowledge Sharing Lessons

Lesson 1. Theory

Within knowledge sharing theory we maintain two primary principles, learn from people and about people and gain the advantages of a rigorous process of questioning.

1.1 Learn from People and About People

The knowledge sharing principle of learning from people and about people argues the view that when individuals with diverse learning resource development objectives and responsibilities meet they must share ideas and achieve an encompassing understanding of one another's intentions, expectations, and requirements.

Learn From People

Throughout the tutorial a principle thought is that every individual though varied in experience, abilities, and education is a valuable asset within evolving learning resource deliberations.

When undertaking learning resource projects it is essential we gain the benefit of individual experience and insights. Examination of failed learning resource projects often reveals that one or more key figures were not included in deliberations, or were not listened to, or listened to too late, and that there were no means in place for individuals to critique decision outcomes, to assess the effect of one decision on others.

Further, learn from people and you discover the roadblocks and bottlenecks that often make new thoughts and new technology difficult to introduce, such as the conflicts of interests created by organizational pressures, group allegiances, differences in intentions, inflexible rules, funding and resource allocation disputes, and political and between organizations controversy.

Learn About People

Learning about people is as important as learning from people. When we work with individuals we not only listen to what they say, we also consider the social and cultural factors that influence their experience and insights, expectations and requirements.

Further, within nations and internationally cultural bias is a factor that must never be overlooked in learning resource project deliberations. A particular area of concern is the fact that the worth and dignity of diverse cultural traditions are often judged in terms of a one's own culture and as a result we ignore, misinterpret, distort or undervalue the contributions of others.

1.2 Rigorous Process of Questioning

How do we learn from people and about people? Within knowledge sharing theory, method, and process a rigorous process of questioning is the bridge between people. It is the core of the knowledge sharing method; particularly important for the exchange of information across cultures. P In knowledge sharing tutorial sessions, working with individuals or groups, we use questions to define the evolving learning resource challenge, and then guide the search for answers within the knowledge sharing process

Within a rigorous process of questioning we see questions as the basis of critical thinking and thorough analysis, the means to discover the exceptions that confound what has been accepted as true. In the knowledge sharing process rigorous questioning takes these forms:

❖ **Discovery.** Questions that consider possibilities and problems, follow insights, and respond to suspicions that something is missing or may be mischaracterized.

❖ **Verification.** Questions designed to confirm data, information, and deliberation outcomes.

❖ **Research.** Questions designed to obtain new data and information and define learning resource requirements and specifications.

Rigorous Process of Questioning Direct and Indirect Benefits

The direct benefits of rigorous questioning are notable:

❖ Questions are fundamental to leadership.

❖ Questions provide an opportunity for debate and argument.

❖ Questions convey your way of managing and thinking.

❖ Questions bring in the next good idea.

❖ Questions help you understand new situations.

❖ Questions make decision-making an open process.

❖ The indirect benefits of rigorous questioning are notable:

❖ Creates a spirit of discovery.

❖ Captures people's attention and interest.

❖ Creates deliberation momentum.

❖ Achieves a commitment to developing new expertise.

❖ Fosters individual consideration of innovation possibilities.

A rigorous process of questioning also shows promise when new issues arise in learning resource projects, requiring we resolve issues in a timely fashion, such as:

- ❖ A last minute requirement or modification.
- ❖ A budget modification.
- ❖ A late discovery of an additional constraint.
- ❖ An overlooked requirement.
- ❖ An organization controversy.

Lesson 2. Method

Excellence in learning and resource achievements relies on a rigorous process of questioning. Here we turn this theory into method in the form of learning resource project deliberation agendas, a framework for critical thinking and thorough analysis.

In terms of providing a background for this overview of the knowledge sharing method, please review the four tutorial studies.

2.1 Deliberation Agendas: Transforming Theory into Method

Knowledge sharing deliberation agendas are designed to gain all the benefits of a rigorous process of questioning, directed to these objectives:

❖ Eliminate unwarranted assumptions and incomplete speculations.

❖ Deal with uncertainty and conflict resolution.

❖ Capture every opportunity and obtain solutions for every problem.

❖ Accumulate ideas and sharpen perceptions and at the same time assure rigorous analysis.

❖ Guard against unwarranted, misdirected, and premature application of concepts and recommendations.

❖ Establish justified and mutually agreed upon learning project intentions, and expectations, requirements, and action plans.

Effectively Employable Deliberation Agendas

Knowledge sharing deliberation agendas promote discovery, clarification, and verification by means of an inclusive process of argument and shared responsibility that assures people discuss the appropriate things; that what might be misunderstood or ignored is clarified and appreciated; and that the time spent on deliberations and research produces exceptional results.

Unlike common organization decision-making that too often predetermines outcomes, reduces the complexity of problems, and limits the scope of solutions, knowledge sharing deliberation participants experiment with ideas and possibilities as related to the following points:

❖ When presented with a question item-based deliberation agenda an individual begins to contribute immediately, putting what he or she knows to work; encouraged to feel free to state that they know something other people do not know or do not understand and to suggest innovations that perhaps only they are capable of conceiving and justifying.

❖ Within this spirit of discovery, deliberation participants have an opportunity to consider what underlies people's intentions, expectations, and requirements, conduct a thorough critique of findings and recommendations, and, in time, revise, expand, and add new topics to project objectives.

The Knowledge Sharing Deliberation Experience

Knowledge sharing deliberations assure that people discuss the appropriate things; that what might be misunderstood or ignored is clarified and appreciated; and that the time spent on project deliberations and research produces exceptional performance and results. In the knowledge sharing method:

❖ Each participant develops his or her own scope of work by selecting from the deliberation agenda question items to which they wish to direct their attention.

❖ Project relevant findings are derived as participants respond to select deliberation agenda question items and the work of others as structured by the online site worksheet and analysis forms.

❖ In the deliberation process all deliberation agenda question items are opened at the beginning of the application and stay open throughout the learning resource development project. Providing an opportunity to extend the level of participation and ask those last questions, which can often enhance results markedly. In this process, statements entered by an individual are open to critique by all participants.

❖ The deliberation agenda is not a step-by-step program. Although deliberation agendas are indexed in a numerical sequence, this does not indicate a sequential application of the question items. Rather than thinking of a starting point and an ending point, think in terms of each deliberation participant following her or his thoughts.

❖ The agenda question-item inventory becomes increasingly more specific during deliberations as question items are revised, expanded, and new questions added by the men and women participating in the deliberation.

❖ Within the deliberation process detailed records of deliberations are maintained; structured as mutually exclusive "addresses" for each question item in the deliberation agenda; identified by unique index number and question item title.

Developing Knowledge Sharing Deliberation Agendas

Continuing on, as simple as any deliberation agenda question item might be the resulting answers can be lengthy and complex, raising the possibility that questions asked might complicate a learning resource project, rather than making it better understood. This is not the case. The formulated learning resource project deliberation agenda provide the "road map" that assures that the benefits of individual experience and insight is realized in an organized fashion.

To make deliberation agendas effectively employable, the learning resource project deliberation agenda:

❖ Must be understandable by the full spectrum of project participants, clear in purpose and requirements.

❖ Must be divided into mutually exclusive critical success factors, allowing a number of individuals to conduct a variety of project deliberations simultaneously.

❖ Must be seen as a scope of work that can be estimated in terms of man-hours needed. Certainly, project deliberations must be reasonable in terms of time, funds, and personnel limitations.

❖ Must provide a means for deliberation history retention. Deliberation agendas are an investment whose benefits must be realized again and again. Learning resource development and management is a recurring phenomenon. Recognizing this repetition, what you learn from one project provides a good beginning for the next project.

2.2 Knowledge Sharing Method Standard of Performance

When you maintain the knowledge sharing method standard

of performance you are taking another step forward in gaining the benefit of individual experience and insights within evolving learning resource deliberations.

The standard of performance for knowledge sharing within learning resource projects is complete, verified, and applicable, and timely knowledge acquisition, where:

❖ **Complete** compares the array of findings with project objectives suggesting where additional deliberations are required.

❖ **Verified** refers to the degree of error in a finding suggesting where additional study is required. Evaluation is not exclusionary, as there will always be an exceptional finding that does not meet evaluation criteria but is retained for consideration because it suggests a promising possibility.

❖ **Applicable** considers results preliminary until evaluated for learning resource project utility; considering at the same time that although a finding appears complete, verified, and applicable, another equally valid finding may tell us something different; a matter to be studied.

❖ **Timely** refers specifically to meeting the project time line. However, alert to the likelihood that a finding will change over time as new points of view are found to exist, we keep in mind it is never too late to seek that final bit of information or reassess a particular deliberation finding.

Critique and Evaluation

Critique and evaluation are an essential part of the knowledge sharing standard of performance, where you consider:

❖ **Interpretation of Findings.** What agreement was reached as to interpretations of findings?

- ❖ **Alternative Interpretations.** What alternative interpretations of findings where given?

- ❖ **Unresolved Issues.** What are the unresolved issues?

- ❖ **Additional Deliberations.** Were additional deliberations undertaken to assess disputed findings?

- ❖ **Concerns and Controversies.** Have significant concerns and controversies been isolated from deliberation findings?

Another Step Forward

The knowledge sharing standard of performance is a response to the shortcomings associated with common information gathering methods ↓ focus groups, lessons learned, brain storming, questionnaires, rating scales, chat rooms, and threaded discussions. And unfortunately, consultants brought in from the outside who too often bias and predetermine outcomes, reduce the complexity of problems, and limit the scope of solutions, and, finally, meetings that too often bias and predetermine outcomes, reduce the complexity of problems, limit the scope of solutions, and do not provide participants time to reflect, gather supporting in formation, and confer with colleagues.

Lesson 3. Process

Building on the tutorial theory and method lessons, this lesson provides guidelines for managing the knowledge sharing process and designing the online deliberation site.

3.1 Managing the Knowledge Sharing Process

When managing a project-specific knowledge sharing process, the following defines the process critical success factors and scope of work ranging from "defining the learning resource project" to "building the knowledge sharing deliberation agenda" to " evaluation of deliberation findings and outcomes".

The following is a worksheet, a guideline for developing and managing a project-specific knowledge sharing process:

1.0 Defining the Learning Resource Project

1.1 **PROJECT CONCEPT.** What is the conceptual definition of the learning resource project to which the knowledge sharing process is directed?

1.2 **PROJECT OBJECTIVES.** What are the learning resource project objectives?

1.3 **CRITICAL SUCCESS FACTORS.** Drawing from the history of the subject-project and associated documents and pertaining professional and research publications and references defining the factors that characterize the learning resource development, what are the project critical success factors?

1.4 **PROJECT RESEARCH.** What is the research activities needed to develop the learning resource project?

1.5 **PROJECT DEVELOPMENT TIMELINE.** What is the sequence of events and schedule for the learning resource project development?

1.6 **PROJECT REDIRECTION.** What situations or events might lead to the modification or redirection of the learning resource project objectives?

2.0 Building the Deliberation Agenda

2.1 **PROJECT DELIBERATION AGENDA.** What objectives should be included in the project deliberation agenda?

2.2 **QUESTION ITEM INVENTORY.** For each project critical success factor what are the defining question-items?

2.3 **PROJECT DELIBERATION AGENDA.** While the question item inventories mirror the project critical success factors scope, not all question items may be included in the project deliberation agenda, therefore: what question items should be included in the project-specific deliberation agenda?

2.4 **DELIBERATION PHASES.** To help participants maintain a sense of purpose and direction, how should the deliberation agenda be arranged by phase and agenda sections?

3.0 Conducting Deliberations

3.1 **PARTICIPATING COMMUNITIES OF INTEREST.** What communities of interest should participate in the knowledge sharing deliberations?

3.2 **INITIAL PARTICIPANTS.** Who should be invited to participate in initial deliberations?

3.3 **ADDITIONAL PARTICIPANTS.** Considering sources of on-the-job and professional and managerial knowledge that are not directly associated with the learning resource development project: What organizations and individuals should be invited to participate in deliberations?

3.4 **NON-PARTICIPANTS**. If individuals and groups were not available for participation, is this noted?

3.5 **DELIBERATION MILESTONE EVENTS AND SCHEDULE**. What are the deliberation phases, outcome milestones, and schedule?

3.6 **INFORMATION SECURITY FEATURES**. Responding to project information security mandates what are the essential online system features.

3.7 **APPLICATION HISTORY**. How should the record of deliberations be arranged for inclusion in the knowledge sharing application archive?

4.0 Designing the Project Deliberation Site

4.1 **DESIGNING THE PROJECT DELIBERATION SITE**. What site features and elements are required to support deliberations?

4.2 **SITE INFORMATION PAGES**. In the context of the current project, what information should be included in Project Description, Participants' Guidelines, and Project Deliberation Agenda?

4.3 **PARTICIPANTS' WORKSHEET AND FINDINGS ANALYSIS FORMS**. How should participants' worksheet and findings analysis forms and site links be designed?

5.0 Deliberation Findings

Critique and evaluation are an essential part of deliberations. These are the questions you pose to evaluate deliberation findings:

5.1 **INTERPRETATION OF FINDINGS**. What agreement was reached as to interpretations of findings?

5.2 **ALTERNATIVE INTERPRETATIONS**. What alternative interpretations of findings are given?

5.3 **UNRESOLVED ISSUES**. What are the unresolved issues?

5.4 **ADDITIONAL DELIBERATIONS**. Where additional deliberations undertaken to assess disputed findings?

5.5 **CONCERNS AND CONTROVERSIES**. Have significant concerns and controversies been identified in deliberation findings?

5.6 **SOURCES OF CONCERNS AND CONTROVERSIES**. Were specific individuals identified as favoring one side or the other of a controversy or expressed concerns?

5.6 **ANECDOTAL STATEMENTS**. Were anecdotal statements identified as such?

6.0 Deliberation Outcomes

6.1 **PROJECT ALTERNATIVES**. Based on deliberation findings what are the learning resource project features and options alternatives?

6.2 **EVALUATING PROJECT ALTERNATIVES**. To what degree do learning resource project alternatives effectively meet the project's critical success factors?

6.3 **RECOMMENDED PROJECT FEATURES**. After alternatives evaluation, what are the features of the recommended learning resource project?

6.4 **JUSTIFICATION FOR RECOMMENDATIONS**. What are the implications of not responding to the recommended learning resource project features?

6.5 **RECOMMENDATION IMPACT**. What aspects of the recommended learning resource project require substantial accommodation on the part of organizations and assigned personnel?

6.6 **IMPACT ON OTHER PROJECTS**. What is the impact of the recommendations on other organization learning resource projects?

6.7 **COST ANALYSIS**. What are the costs associated with

recommended learning resource project features and associated requirements?

6.8 **INCORPORATING EVOLVING TECHNOLOGY.** Where and in what manner is evolving ICT technology incorporated into the learning resource project?

6.9 **TRANSITION CONCERNS.** What are the organization challenges in terms of transition to the recommended learning resource project features?

6.10 **EXISTING CONCERNS.** What are the organization's concerns regarding the possible adverse impact of the recommended learning resource project?

6.11 **NEW SKILLS.** Responding to the proposed learning resource project what new skills will people need?

6.12 **ADDITIONAL DELIBERATIONS.** What additional deliberations are needed to confirm learning resource recommendations?

6.13 **IMPROVING THE RECOMMENDED PROJECT.** Upon review of recommended learning resource project, where can concepts and features be improved?

6.14 **ANTICIPATED CHANGE.** Looking ahead, what events may require further attention to the recommended learning resource project?

6.15 **APPLYING FINDINGS TO OTHER PROJECTS.** Considering deliberation findings, what has been learned that may prove valuable to other learning resource projects?

3.2 Knowledge Sharing Site Design

The knowledge sharing site design objective is to enable the process plan developed in the preceding section, 3.1 Managing the Knowledge Sharing Process. Two additions to this topic follow: knowledge sharing site experience and a site design guideline.

To gain information and communication technology advantages for supporting the knowledge sharing site experience the following provides the starting point for site development work.

Site Program Selection

The knowledge sharing experience is enabled by programs such as *Microsoft's* SharePoint , *Adobe's* Acrobat Professional and Readers programs, and SendNow Desktop project linking e-mail service.

The *Teamwork Project Manager* programs and services are particularly valuable; providing a dedicated knowledge sharing website making available knowledge sharing history, lists, libraries, links, and all the entries and dialogues associated deliberation agenda. This program provides a dedicate web site that can be found and opened directly within available search programs.

Responsibilities

Site features are developed in response to knowledge sharing participants' responsibilities.

Deliberation Leaders' Responsibilities

Deliberation leaders are individuals appointed to facilitate the work of project deliberation participants and develop and maintain the project deliberation agenda and site. Their primary responsibilities are:

- ❖ Introduce the objectives of each phase of the deliberation agenda, an initiative-specific guideline for participants.
- ❖ Oversee the application and communicate with deliberation participants' areas of concern.
- ❖ Authorize site access where information security measures are mandated.

Participants' Responsibilities

Participants are the men and women who contribute to project deliberations. The primary responsibility of deliberation participants is to:

- ❖ Apply their initiative, experience, and, insight to the questions they select to answer or are asked to answer by the application leaders.

- ❖ Critique the analyses of findings and recommendations developed by deliberation participants.

- ❖ Suggest new question items for consideration.

- ❖ Recommend action in terms of deliberation findings or what they see as promising possibilities.

Participants' Worksheet Forms

Participants use two deliberation entry forms, Worksheet and Finding Analysis. For deliberations to be successful the graphic user interface that guides the deliberation process must be readily understood. The notable features are:

- ❖ The forms are designed so that all entries are directed to a specific deliberation agenda question item.

- ❖ All entries are tagged with the name and organization of the contributing participant.

- ❖ Large work areas, full word processing utilities, and no limit to length of text entries characterize all the entry forms.

- ❖ The forms accept referenced files and hyperlinks.

The worksheet form is the participant's main work area. A selected question item is the topic with three parts to the form. **Comments.** This is where participants express what they consider the important aspects of the subject question item. **Recommendations**. The second part of the form is for statements of proposed action and judgments concerning enterprise intentions, expectations, and requirements. **Suggested New Question Items**. This is where participants propose new question items. Other participants review these. When recognized as an important contribution the proposed item is added to the learning resource project deliberation agenda inventory.

Participants' Findings Analysis Form

Participants use this form to analyze findings; results are reviewed by deliberation participants and associated communities of interest. **Significance of Findings** is first part of the form. **Recommendations** are made in the second part of the form is in the context of the implication of findings for learning resource project intentions, expectations, and requirements,

Application History

Applying information and communication technology advantages the entire deliberation can be reconstructed. The pathway from outcome statements of intentions, expectations, and requirements can be traced to contributing individuals and the deliberations associated with specific question items. These records from undertaking to undertaking can be compiled into an archive; a significant resource when new knowledge sharing applications.

Site Navigation Scheme

The following elements identify required knowledge sharing site pages and links:

Project Information Pages

Project History and Objectives

Participants' Deliberation Responsibilities

Knowledge Sharing Tutorial e-Book

Introduction to Site Features

Project Deliberation Agenda

Use Guidelines for Worksheets and Findings Analysis Forms

Project Document and References

Site Links Index

Participants' Identity, Organization, and e-Mail Address

Project Deliberation Agenda Access

Participants' Worksheet Entries

Participants' Analysis Outcomes

Record of Deliberation Findings

Project Deliberation History Archive

3.3 Managing the Knowledge Sharing Site

Deliberation leaders determine the initial direction of deliberations; and orchestrate the contributions of participants to achieve desired outcomes and effort. Participants may be directed to an entire deliberation agenda or selected critical success factors.

Do not consider the deliberation agenda a step-by-step program. It is important to remember that although deliberation agendas are organized in a numerical sequence, this does not indicate a sequential application of the question items. Rather than thinking of a starting point and an ending point, think in terms of each deliberation participant following her or his thoughts; deliberation online site features provide for this.

Within the process detailed records of deliberations are maintained; structured by the mutually exclusive "address" for each question item in the deliberation agenda; identified by unique index number and question item title. In the Process all deliberation agenda question items are opened at the beginning of the application and stay open throughout the undertaking. There is always an opportunity to extend the level of participation and ask those last questions, which can often enhance results markedly. In this process, statements entered by an individual are open to critique by all participants.

Knowledge Sharing Process Review

The knowledge sharing process provides essential support for learning resource development deliberations:

- ❖ The knowledge sharing online site supports an activity where participating individuals and workgroups view and contribute to the same document and work with no time or location constraints and where people share critical questions and points of view.

- ❖ Ease-of-use online site design features help make learning resource project participants active thinkers, as opposed to passive participants who offer little that goes beyond established data and information. Online site features provide identity to all entries made; encouraging the feeling that a personal view is valuable.

- ❖ Online site features provide a means to evaluate findings, formulate recommendations, and provide justification for recommendations and proposed action.

❖ A notable advantage of site information and communication technology is the ease with which numbers of participants can be selectively increased to infuse deliberations with new perspectives. What must be appreciated is that unlike meetings online deliberation provides individuals time to reflect, confer with colleagues, and gather supporting documents.

The following reviews the deliberations agenda and knowledge sharing online site protocols:

❖ Having placed the developed deliberation agenda in an online site, deliberations begin with an introduction to the learning resource objectives and deliberation protocols. This presentation must energize participants. Deliberation participants must appreciate what they are being asked to do and appreciate the sense of shared responsibility for initiative success.

❖ Deliberations begin when each participant develops his or her own scope of work by selecting from the deliberation agenda question items to which they wish to direct their attention.

❖ Application findings are derived as participants respond to selected question items and the work of others as structured by the site worksheet and analysis forms.

❖ The site protocol specifies that each form entry is directed to a specific question item and that each entry is tagged by the originator's name and organization.

❖ A complete record of site deliberations and findings is maintained and available on-line to the executives, managers, and associates of the learning resource development initiative.

❖ Deliberation on-line site features provide a means for deliberation participants and leaders to highlight deliberation findings, state the significance of findings, formulate recommendations, and provide justification for recommendations and proposed action.

Part II. Knowledge Sharing Studies

Study 1. Evolving School Learning Resources, Introducing New Thoughts and New Technology

Study 2. Building for the Future, A Promising Community Learning Center Opportunity

Study 3. Continuous Workforce Improvement, A Challenging Problem for Personalized Learning

Study 4. A Knowledge Sharing Research Strategy, Directed to Changing Social and Economic Conditions

In the context of knowledge sharing theory, method, and process these studies answering this question: How can we develop effective knowledge sharing experiences within evolving learning resources?

In the knowledge sharing studies the answer will be increasingly more positive as people recognize that the knowledge sharing experience complements their expertise, experience, and insights—a means to achieve a dramatic improvement in opportunities for participants in a learning resource development project to exchange insights and points of view, evaluate intentions and requirements, and gain access to pertinent information that too often escapes attention.

Study 1. Evolving School Learning Resources, Introducing New thoughts and New Technology

This study shows how the knowledge sharing experience provides the best possible start for educators working to achieve their information and communication technology (ICT) resources vision; taking measures to define and enhance the learning experience and respond to individual, family, and community needs.

The study deliberation agenda provides a means to identify the range of interests that often make new thoughts and new technology difficult to introduce as you are challenged by education staff and teachers varying points of view, personal allegiances, differences in intentions, inflexible rules, funding and resource allocation disputes, and political and community controversy.

An insight to kept in mind: Dr. Balint Magyar, *Minister of Education, Hungary*, cautions…. that the appearance of technological wonders and their use in the field of education cannot automatically be regarded as pedagogical innovation. The employment of technical resources is not necessarily a satisfactory condition for innovative practice, it can serve only to support, assist or elicit innovation.

Study Deliberation Agenda

Supporting evolving ICT learning resource objectives, the study emphasizes it is essential that the following communities of interest work with a sense of shared responsibility and gain the benefit of individual experience and insights:

- ❖ Educators developing learning resources associated with information and communication technical advantages.
- ❖ Communities and neighborhoods dedicated to student opportunity and achievement.
- ❖ Community and neighborhood entities expressing concerns associated with student, family, ethnic, and cultural diversity.
- ❖ School administrators and education boards responding to diverse community interests and expectations.

Deliberation Agenda Index

Part 1. First Steps: Establishing the ICT Initiative

As the work opens, the initiative leaders review, select from, edit, and augment the question items presented in this resource deliberation agenda to establish the initial scope of their collective effort. The agenda becomes increasingly more initiative-specific as question items are revised, expanded, and new questions added.

1.0 Learning ICT-based Initiative Concept

1.1 **INITIATIVE CONCEPT.** What is the initiative ICT-based learning concept?

1.2 **INITIATIVE OBJECTIVES.** What are the ICT initiative objectives?

1.3 **INTIATIVE'S CRITICAL SUCESS FACTORS.** What are the ICT initiative critical success factors?

2.0 Initial Deliberation Participants

2.1 **DELIBERATION LEADERS.** What organizations and communities of interest should be asked to appoint deliberation leaders?

2.2 **INITIAL PARTICIPANTS.** For initial deliberations who should be invited to participate?

2.3 **ADDITIONAL INITIATIVE PARTICIPANTS.** When new sources of expertise and experience are required who should be invited to participate in initiative deliberations?

2.4 **UNIVERSITY PARTICIPATION.** How can universities be of assistance in the development of the ICT-based learning curricula?

2.5 **INTERNATIONAL, NATIONAL, AND REGIONAL ENTITIES.** How can international, national, and regional entities be of assistance in the development of ICT-based learning curricula?

3.0 Initiative Deliberation Agenda

3.1 **BUILDING THE INITIATIVE DELIBERATION AGENDA.** What initiative objectives and critical success factors should be addressed and formulated into question items for inclusion into the deliberation agenda?

3.2 **INITIATIVE CRITICAL SUCCESS FACTORS.** Drawing from the archives of professional and research publications, what is the initiative knowledge domain?

3.3 **QUESTION ITEM INVENTORY.** For each knowledge domain information category what are the defining question items?

3.4 **INITIATIVE DELIBERATION AGENDA.** While the question-item inventory mirrors the knowledge domain scope, not all question items may be included in the initiative deliberation agenda, therefore: what items should be included in the initiative deliberation agenda?

4.0 Designing the Project Online Site

4.1 **DELIBERATION SITE**. What are the required deliberation online site features and protocols?

4.2 **HOME PAGE**. What information should be linked to site Home page, such as Initiative Description, Deliberation Participants' Guidelines, Tutorial Lessons, and References?

4.3 **DELIBERATION AGENDA PRESENTATION**. To help participants maintain a sense of purpose and direction, how should the deliberation agenda and supporting comments be organized for presentation?

4.4 **PARTICIPANTS' WORKSHEET AND FEEDBACK FORMS**. How should participants' Worksheet and Feedback forms be designed?

4.5 **DELIBERATION LEADERS' FORMS**. How should deliberation leaders' forms be designed?

Part 2. Learning About the Evolving ICT-based Curricula

The transition from traditional educational environments to the introduction of new thoughts and new technology is a challenging undertaking. Deliberations are seldom free of uncertainty and controversy. This is expected when you consider the conflicts of interests created by what is important to individuals with different responsibilities and experience, organizational pressures, community allegiances, and pedagogical philosophy.

5.0 ICT-Based Learning Curricula Aspects

5.1 **ICT-BASED LEARNING ALTERNATIVES AND OPTIONS**. Responding to the initiative concept, objectives, and critical success factors, what are the ICT-based learning curricula alternatives and options?

5.2 **TEACHING METHODS INNOVATIONS**. To successfully establish the ICT-based learning curricula, what innovations in teaching methods should be considered?

5.3 **TEACHER QUALIFICATIONS**. What are the educational and experience qualifications for teachers participating in the ICT-based learning curricula?

5.4 **STUDENT DIVERSITY**. Considering student cultural and social diversity, what features of the ICT-based learning curricula require special attention?

5.5 **LIMITED ICT EXPERIENCE CONSIDERATIONS**. How should the learning curricula be crafted to meet the needs of students with limited ICT experience?

5.6 **LEARNING READINESS**. What characteristics can be used in to define student readiness for the ICT learning curricula?

6.0 Essential ICT Requirements

6.1 **ICT ADVANTAGES**. In what way can ICT advantages be used to meet learning curricula expectations and requirements?

6.2 **ICT OPERATIONAL SYSTEM AND SOFTWARE**. Considering the teacher and student learning-related activities, what are the ICT operational system and software requirements?

6.3 **ICT WORKSTATION FEATURES**. What are the furnishing, equipment, and fixture requirements for ICT workstations?

6.4 **WORKSTATION LOCATIONS**. Where should workstations be located to assure the best possible security and efficient activities?

6.5 **FACILITY REQUIREMENTS**. What are the facility requirements associated with the ICT learning curricula?

6.6 **PROFESSIONAL AND TECHNICAL RESOURCES**. What professional and technical resources are needed to maintain the ICT system?

6.7 **PERFORMANCE EVALUATIONS**. What evaluations are needed to confirm ICT design features?

6.8 **INTERNET NETWORK.** A feature of ICT-based learning is internet links to student, home, and community; how can this be achieved?

6.9 **ADDITIONAL ICT PROFESSIONAL AND TECHNICAL PARTICIPANTS.** Who knows a great deal about essential ICT advantages and should be invited to participate in initiative deliberations?

Part 3. School Administration, Teacher, Student, Parent, and Community Insights

Use the initiative, experience, and knowledge of these deliberation participants to move beyond common professional interests and what the information on hand indicates. When it comes to making recommendations anecdotes are too often omitted. When we limit a position by stressing facts and numerical analysis over individual insight, we leave out what may be most informative.

7.0 School Administration Concerns

7.1 **SCHOOL ADMINISTRATION RESPONSIBILITIES.** Within the ICT-based learning curricula what should be the responsibilities of school administrators?

7.2 **RESOURCE CONCERNS.** What are the concerns of school administrators regarding resource availability for establishing the ICT-based learning curricula?

7.3 **ADDITIONAL ADMINISTRATION PARTICIPANTS.** Who knows a great deal about ICT-based curricula administration and should be invited to participate in initiative deliberations?

8.0 Teachers' Points of View

8.1 **OVERLOOKED EDUCATIONAL OBJECTIVES.** Are there educational objectives that have been overlooked during deliberations?

8.2 **OVERLOOKED TEACHER ACTIVITIES**. What teacher activities are overlooked within the initiative deliberations?

8.3 **MISLEADING OR INCOMPLETE STATEMENTS**. Within the record of deliberations are there misleading or incomplete statements?

8.4 **ALTERNATIVE INTERPRETATIONS**. What alternative interpretations of findings within the record of deliberations would you like to suggest?

8.5 **UNRESOLVED ISSUES**. Have you identified unresolved ICT-based learning issues?

8.6 **POINTS OF VIEW**. What are teachers' views about the ICT-based learning curricula?

8.7 **TRANSITION CHALLENGE**. What are the challenges facing teachers in terms of transition to the ICT-based learning curricula?

8.8 **STUDENT ACHIEVEMENT BENEFITS**. What ICT-based learning curricula features will have notable student achievement benefits?

8.9 **OVERLOOKED STUDENT OPPORTUNITIES**. What student opportunities are overlooked within initiative deliberations?

8.10 **STUDENTS WITH LIMITED ABILITIES**. What is needed to help students with limited learning abilities to succeed within the ICT-based learning curricula?

8.11 **IMPACT ON NORMS, CUSTOMS, AND TRADITIONS**. What is the anticipated impact of the ICT-based learning curricula on the social customs, relationship norms, and cultural traditions of the school and students, parents, and the community?

8.12 **TEACHER AND PARENT RELATIONS**. What views exist regarding the impact of the ICT-based learning curricula on the relationships between teachers and parents?

8.13 **VOLUNTEER MENTORS**. How important is the role of volunteer mentors in helping the ICT-based learning curricula meet the needs of students?

8.14 **ADDITIONAL PROFESSIONAL PARTICIPANTS.** Who knows a great deal about ICT-based self-guided learning curricula and should be invited to participate in deliberations?

9.0 Student Insights

9.1 **STUDENT INTERESTS.** What will the opportunity for ICT-Based learning mean to you?

9.2 **OPPORTUNITIES.** Where would you like to see ICT-Based learning opportunities established?

9.3 **BEFORE AND AFTER-SCHOOL OPPORTUNITIES.** How important is it that the school provides before and after-school ICT-based learning opportunities?

9.4 **ANTICIPATED PROBLEMS.** Where do you think the ICT-based learning is going to be a problem for you?

9.5 **CURRICULUM SHORTCOMINGS.** What should be done to improve the ICT-based learning curricula?

9.6 **ADDITIONAL STUDENT PARTICIPANTS.** What other students should be invited to evaluate initiative deliberations?

10.0 Parents' Points of View

10.1 **SHORTSIGHTED THINKING.** In terms of the deliberation record, where do you think people are shortsighted about what is best for your child?

10.2 **CONCERNS.** Where are you concerned that your child will be disadvantaged by the demands associated with the ICT-based learning curricula?

10.3 **ADDITIONAL PARENT PARTICIPANTS.** What parents have good ideas about improving the students' educational experience and should be invited to participate in initiative deliberations?

11.0 Community Interests

11.1 **LIFELONG LEARNING.** How can the school's ICT-based learning expertise be used to support local businesses and corporation and government entities interested in lifelong learning opportunities?

11.2 **COMMUNITY PERSPECTIVES.** Where does the ICT-based learning curricula require refinement in terms of community concerns, social conditions, and resources?

11.3 **ECONOMIC DEVELOPMENT PLAN.** Does the ICT-based learning initiative have a role within the community's economic development plan?

11.4 **FINANCIAL SUPPORT.** What steps can be taken to attract financial support for the ICT-based learning initiative from local businesses and corporations and government entities?

11.5 **ADDITIONAL COMMUNITY PARTICIPANTS.** Who knows a great deal about ICT advantages and should be invited to participate in initiative deliberations?

Part 4: Establishing Curriculum Intentions, Expectations, and Requirements

12.0 ICT Deliberation Outcomes

12.1 **ICT-BASED LEARNING CURRICULA ALTERNATIVES.** Based on an analysis of deliberation findings what are the ICT-based learning curricula alternatives and options?

12.2 **EVALUATING ICT-BASED LEARNING CURRICULA ALTERNATIVES.** To what degree does each ICT-based learning curricula alternative fulfill the desired teacher and student educational experience?

12.3 **THE RECOMMENDED ICT-BASED LEARNING CURRICULA.** In terms of alternatives evaluation, what are the recommended ICT-based learning curricula?

12.4 **JUSTIFICATION FOR RECOMMENDATION**. What is the justification for the recommended ICT-based learning curricula?

12.5 **COST ANALYSIS**. What are the costs associated with the recommended ICT-based learning curricula?

12.6 **SCHOOL ADMINISTRATION CONCERNS**. How can school administration's concerns about the recommended ICT-based learning curricula be reduced or eliminated?

12.7 **TEACHER AND STUDENTS IMPACT**. What aspects of the recommended ICT-based learning require substantial accommodation on the part of the teachers and students?

12.8 **TRANSITION PLANNING**. What are the solutions for reducing the adverse impact of the transition to the recommended ICT-based learning curricula?

12.9 **NEW SKILLS**. Responding to recommended ICT-based learning curricula what new skills within the school organization are needed?

12.10 **ADDITIONAL DELIBERATIONS**. What additional deliberations are needed to confirm the ICT-based learning curricula recommendation?

12.11 **CONTINUAL EVALUATION**. Once the ICT-based learning curricula are established what evaluation program should be put in place to assess progress and identify possibilities for curricula improvement?

12.12 **ADDITIONAL CONCLUDING PHRASE PARTICIPANTS**. Who should be invited to conduct a critique of the recommended ICT-based learning curricula?

Study 2. Building for the Future, A Promising Community Learning Center Opportunity

In this knowledge sharing study a community development committee is charged to identify promising opportunities for advancing community economic growth. Considering the future, the gaining of economic benefits, new employment opportunities, and enhanced community identity that draws investments and business development to the community the committee proposed a Community Learning Center enterprise.

Responsive to knowledge sharing theory, method, and process, the three parts of this study are Part I. Community Learning Center Objectives, Part II. Working Relations with Center Designers and Contractors, and Part III. Enterprise Knowledge Sharing Deliberation Agenda.

Part I. Community Learning Center Objectives

After discussing their proposal with university of technology and economics faculty, business interests, and government agencies, the committee defined the Community Learning Center enterprise specific objectives, in terms of answering this question: Who will be served by the Community Learning Center? The result of this preliminary work defines the Community Learning Center enterprise objectives.

Business and Government Subscribers

Subscription membership in the Community Learning Center provides space and information and communication technology (ICT) support for start-up businesses, business and professional firms, and corporate and government entities.

Professional Education and Technical Training Subscribers

Within the Community Learning Center facility space and ICT support is provided for technical training and professional education programs. Space and services are provided for courses, conferences, seminars, and private meetings and special events for grammar school to university student groups.

Community Human Resource Development Alliance

In alliance with community human services the Community Learning Center supports and provides programs and training facilities for the physically disabled, educationally disadvantaged, mentally less able, and the elderly requiring work skill development.

Center Services

The center services are scheduled to be open 24 hours a day, 7 days a week. The Community Learning Center services are extensive, including:

- ❖ An information and communication technology library, and a business development center supporting new products and markets research and development undertakings.
- ❖ Center concessions including restaurants, book and office supplies stores, and ICT sales and service businesses.
- ❖ Center operations support ranging from facility and ICT

maintenance staff to security force, center receptionists, and parking attendants.

Part II. Working Relations with Center Designers and Contractors

From the very beginning of the enterprise the community development committee considered their working relations with center designers and contractors.

Preparing for this, the enterprise committee studied guidelines, such as the *Royal Institute of British Architects Building for the Future Guide,* designed to help communities negotiate their way through complex building initiatives, recognizing as the daily life of people is becoming more complex, the need for perfected facilities is becoming more essential.

The community development committee recognized now is the time to consider contracts for design and construction firms. Considering contract award, the enterprise requires professional designers and construction managers known for developing exceptional building features and performance, gaining full value from the construction dollar—people who will work with community representatives to employ their insights and experience, a strategy encouraging exceptional quality of life environments.

The design and construction firms selected need graphic modeling capabilities. Where we see building information modeling as a means to bring life to a building before there is a building. Which is what people mean when they use the term "virtual reality".

Part III. Enterprise Knowledge Sharing Deliberation Agenda

Knowledge sharing is a strategy for success, which benefits

from the shared responsibility experiences of the community and design and construction professionals.

There is no question that the expertise, experience, and insights of community members are too often underutilized in such projects as the Community Learning Center enterprise. Within this study the community participates in deliberations helping determine the aspects of the Community Learning Center objectives, expectations, and requirements that are particularly important and require extensive facility service and design consideration.

Once the center design and construction team is formed, the community representatives will participate in facility design deliberations. Design evaluation by community representatives is essential to ensuring success.

In the context of the enterprise objectives specified in Part I., who will be served by the Community Learning Center, the community development committee and design and construction team developed a ten- element knowledge sharing deliberation agenda.

The first element, 1.0 Interior Architectural Spaces, begins the development of the facility schemes, forms, and features needed to support center subscriber, staff, and concession activities. The second element, 2.0 Critical Circulation Patterns, begins with a study of facility user movements and equipment and material transport. It concludes with the specification of recommended facility circulation patterns. In the next element, 3.0 Individuals with Physical and Sensory Disabilities, the goal is to identify situations that require customized furnishing, fixtures, equipment, and space features. The fourth element, 4.0 Center ICT Workstations, is an increasingly important design consideration. Facility design features must support ICT requirements and information development and processing activities.

When the fifth agenda element, 5.0 Facility Space Arrangements, is reached, sufficient information exists to create floor plan schemes, options and alternatives, and associated facility management guidelines. The 6.0 Facility Design Image element provides standards that serve to guide the development of exterior and interior design image features. The seventh element, 7.0 Facility Site Planning guides the achievement of compatibility between facility and site in terms of anticipated activities.

The last three deliberation agenda elements, 8.0 Financial Analysis, 9.0 Outcome Evaluation, and 10.0 Refining Design Solutions provide information needed for applying for government grants, community bond issues, and private investments.

All parts of this deliberation agenda are available online, where a record of deliberations and findings is maintained; available to all enterprise community participants and design and construction managers associated with Community Learning Center enterprise.

Knowledge Sharing Deliberation Agenda

From the very beginning of enterprise deliberations building design and construction professionals work to organize and evaluate information, identify design possibilities, and formulate recommendations. The role of community deliberation participants is to critique proposed design features and offer alternative possibilities that will make center design more representative of Community Learning Center objectives, expectations, and requirements.

1.0 Interior Center Spaces

1.1 **SPACE REQUIREMENTS**. What spaces are needed to support center users' activities?

1.2 **FURNISHING, FIXTURES, AND EQUIPMENT ALLOCATIONS**. What furnishing, fixtures, and equipment, fixed or mobile, does each facility space require?

1.3 **SECURITY AND SAFETY**. In anticipation of undesirable and emergency events, what special safety and security measures are necessary?

1.4 **AMBIENT ENVIRONMENTAL CRITERIA**. What provisions should be made for the effect on facility users of temperature, humidity, air quality, air movement, illumination, noise, distractions, annoyances, hazards, and climatic conditions?

1.5 **INFORMATION DISPLAYS**. What are the required information displays?

1.6 **DURABILITY AND MAINTAINABILITY**. Where do spaces require special attention to durability and maintainability of surfaces and furnishings?

1.7 **SPACE PLANS**. What space plans best correspond to facility users' expectations and requirements?

This section of the enterprise deliberation agenda is a specific response to the potential of interior architectural spaces to form the pathway to Community Learning Center a success. Conversely, unsatisfactory interior features can intervene in actions, fail to support important activities, and can be incompatible with scribers' preferred ways of doing things.

Security and safety considerations are included in these deliberations—2.3 SECURITY and SAFETY. In anticipation of undesirable and emergency events, what special safety and security measures are necessary?

This topic is often complex, and may require special study. Security is a concern requiring a complete design strategy that takes into account what must be secure and the associated threat.

Threats to individual security must be described in detail; a mitigating design should then be developed. Patterns of anticipated behavior may lead to emphasizing exterior lighting, individually controlled locking devices, sensors and triggering mechanisms, or even the establishment of a building or neighborhood watch or escort program.

Accidents, fires, earthquakes, and other threats to individual safety certainly require a design response. Establishing escape strategies for fires illustrates this point. The location of signs is one thing; the design of multi-modality information displays that work effectively in smoke occluded spaces and when people are panicked is another. By establishing the best possible means for providing with directions and warnings ahead of time, and supporting this effort with design features, the full potential of facility design and emergency event management is realized.

2.0 Critical Circulation Patterns

The three question items in this section of the Community Learning Center deliberation agenda provide the informational basis for perfecting facility circulation, the movement and flow of people and equipment and material.

For many building designers information that describes the circulation patterns of facility provide essential insights for appropriate facility design schemes. If facility circulation patterns are perfected the likelihood of a successful project is markedly increased.

2.1 **CENTER OCCUPANTS**. How many people will be entering, leaving, and moving about within the center, for what purposes and how frequently?

2.2 **EQUIPMENT AND MATERIAL TRANSPORT**. What are the characteristics of the equipment and material that must be transported to and within the facility? How will these items be transported, and what is the frequency of such movements?

2.3 **RECOMMENDED CIRCULATION PATTERNS**. What are the recommended circulation patterns for user and equipment and material flow? In what way is this proposal a response to concerns for efficiency and convenience, safety, and security?

3.0 Individuals with Physical and Sensory Disabilities

The following question items help keep in mind the importance of facility design features that accommodate the requirements of the physically and sensory disabled.

3.1 **PHYSICALLY DISABLED.** To help assure a safe and convenient experience for center occupants and visitors, what must be done to support people with permanent and temporary physical disabilities?

3.2 **SENSORY DISABLED.** To help assure a safe and convenient experience for center occupants and visitors, what must be done to support people with sensory limitations and disabilities?

3.3 **NEW PRODUCTS AND TECHNOLOGY.** What new products and technology can increase the possibilities for meeting the needs of center occupants and visitors with physical and sensory disabilities?

4.0 Center ICT Workstations

The central feature of the Community Learning Center will be provided ICT workstations that are designed to support specific center programs. These are deliberations that should include potential center subscribers.

4.1 **ICT WORKSTATION FACILITIES.** Where are center workstations required?

4.2 **ICT WORKSTATION ACTIVITIES.** What are the specific workstation activities?

4.3 **ICT WORKSTATION FEATURES.** What are the furnishing requirements of subject workstations?

4.4 **ICT WORKSTATION LAYOUT.** Since each workstation has unique activities and support requirements, how should each workstation be arranged?

4.5 **ICT OPERATING SYSTEMS AND APPLICATIONS**. For center provided ICT workstations, what are essential ICT operating systems and applications?

4.6 **ICT WORKSTATION MANAGEMENT SYSTEM**. What are the necessary guidelines and manuals that help people understand ICT workstation features?

5.0 Facility Space Arrangements

5.1 **PROPOSED FLOOR PLAN SCHEMES**. Considering all research findings and developed design concepts, what are the best schemes for achieving Community Learning Center service and quality of life objectives?

5.2 **SPACE REQUIREMENTS**. What is the estimated square meters/feet for each facility space and support area?

5.3 **ANTICIPATING NEW REQUIREMENTS**. What proposed design features anticipate the need to modify or expand the Corporate Learning Center? What events would most probably lead to this requirement? What can be done to help reduce the distractions and annoyances associated with remodeling and expansion?

These question items emphasize critique and selective modification of proposed design schemes, forms, and features. Research findings and corresponding design recommendations are always placed in the context of such considerations as site constraints, structural systems and materials, construction methods and schedules, and cost analyses. This provides the enterprise design team with a head start on the identification of conflicts and the formulation of compromises.

Question item 5.1 synthesizes findings and provide a summary of the spatial implications for the total design. Many will consider it premature to become so specific this early in design and may wish to formulate a less binding recommendation. Nevertheless, It is essential that the design concepts, schemes, forms, and features are presented for community and subscriber critique, an opportunity in terms of obtaining options and alternatives recommendations. There is always more than one way to meet people's expectations and requirements.

In question item 5.2 Space Requirements a precise calculation of total square meters (feet) for the facility is formulated. Applying a current construction cost index to this calculation provides a preliminary cost estimate. As the building design and land development team reviews these numbers and attempts to reduce costs, deliberations can be augmented with what is known about the significance of each space. Every square meter is supported by a description of associated client and facility user expectations and requirements.

6.0 Center Design Image

6.1 **FORMS AND STRUCTURE**. What are the proposed center forms and structure design concepts?

6.2 **EXTERIOR DESIGN IMAGES**. What are the proposals for exterior center design images, details, and accents?

6.3 **INTERIOR DESIGN IMAGES**. What are the proposals for interior spatial forms, design images, and surface colors, textures and patterns?

6.4 **CONCEPT JUSTIFICATION**. What are the user effects possibilities of each design image recommendation?

What we know about facility life characteristics should be reflected in the work achieved here. The merit of the formulated design guideline is based on the thoroughness of the original research. This sequence of questions will define the main features of the space images. With this model as a reference, the building design and land development team must then consider options and alternatives. Certainly, alternative development is a means of critique. As community participants review preliminary designs, possible controversy will be identified.

7.0 Center Site Plan

7.1 **CENTER SITE REQUIREMENTS**. What are the center site requirements and to what needs and wants do these correspond?

7.2 **OUTDOOR SPACE**. What are the requirements for outdoor space in terms of amenities, landscape development and preservation, and enhancement of existing natural features?

7.3 **AREA IMPACT**. What are the activities surrounding the site? What will be the impact of center activities on the surrounding neighborhoods?

7.4 **SITE PLANS**. How should the site be planned in order to achieve quality of life objectives, respond to the needs of those occupying nearby sites, and meet requirements for outdoor space in terms of amenities and landscape development?

The deliberation participants representing neighborhood and community interests will contribute to the development of site design guidelines. Early in the work of on site design these individuals will help identify existing expectations, concerns, and requirements. As site design features are formed, these individuals will critique and help revise preliminary recommendations.

8.0 Center Financial Analysis

8.1 **FINANCIAL REQUIREMENTS**. What are the financial requirements for the various development phases of the Community Learning Center building project?

8.2 **FUNDING SOURCES**. What are the possible funding sources for the center? What steps must be taken to make the request for funding as competitive and attractive as possible? What questions must be addressed when preparing the funding request?

8.3 **OPERATING COSTS**. What are the anticipated operating costs for the center, prior to occupancy, at occupancy, and over time?

8.4 **ON-SITE REVENUE**. What are the revenue categories and anticipated on-site revenues for the enterprise?

8.5 **GAINING COMMUNITY SUPPORT**. As the Corporate Learning Center enterprise project means jobs and increased economic activity in the local community, what is the best way to present the associated center benefits?

8.6 **ENTERPRISE FEASIBILITY STUDY**. As each of the preceding question items are candidates for inclusion in the Community Learning Center enterprise feasibility study, what is the best possible financial feasibility presentation?

9.0 Outcome Evaluation

9.1 **OVERLOOKED ACTIVITIES**. Is there a Community Learning Center expectation or requirement that has been overlooked?

9.2 **INCORRECT OR INCOMPLETE STATEMENTS**. Is there a Community Learning Center activity description that is incorrect or incomplete?

9.3 **INTERPRETATIONS CRITIQUE**. Were interpretations of deliberation outcomes findings open to question, what are the alternative interpretations of findings?

9.4 **UNRESOLVED ISSUES**. Are there unresolved Community Learning Center enterprise issues?

9.5 **RESOLVING ISSUES**. What steps can be undertaken to resolve Community Learning Center enterprise issues?

10.0 Refining Design Solutions

We want to visually characterize the proposed Community Learning Center features that are regarded as essential for enterprise success. Two and three dimensions graphics convey more meaning with greater clarity than any rhetoric, from which proposed and alternative design features can be understood and evaluated.

Building Information Modeling (BIM) representation of Community Learning Center features and specifications support the refinement of design solutions.

10.1 **BIM SUPPORT**. What Community Learning Center design features and specifications require BIM?

10.2 **BIM EXTENSIVE ATTENTION**. In terms of the role of the BIM-system in center design and construction, where is extensive BIM attention required?

10.3 **EVALUATION PROGRAM**. Procedures must be established to assure that BIM outcomes are evaluated, therefore: What enterprise participants should be given the responsibility for conducting BIM outcomes evaluation?

Study 3. Continuous Workforce Improvement, A Challenging Problem for Personalized Learning

Within manufacturing, service, and marketing organizations what is critical for innovation, productivity, and quality control is a skilled and productive workforce. For this objective corporate, business, institutional, and government managers should consider the value of developing their own personalized learning resources, courses customized to address workforce areas of responsibility.

This personalized learning course is designed to introduce skilled and productive expert knowledge in all its aspects, to understand the responsibilities of the entire workforce, from human resource development to work system design. In the last part of the course syllabus, to apply the expert knowledge domain to a specific area of responsibility; learning to think in terms of confirming the things they know, finding out all they can about what they need to know, and deciding what exploratory research is needed to assure that they discover the things they are unaware of but which may dramatically affect initiative outcomes.

An indirect benefit: When you recognize it is the professional, technical, and service workforce that builds the pathway to success, personalized learning opportunities are a sign of regard for workforce initiative, experience, and insights, a means to accelerate the building of a confident and expert workforce.

Course Mentor's Responsibilities

To achieve skilled and productive learning objectives, the personalized learning mentor's responsibility is to introduce students to expert knowledge in all its dimensions, attaining a complete, thorough, and precise understanding of all the aspects of what is meant by the phrase "skilled and productive". For this objective, the skilled and productive workforce course is divided into two parts: study the skilled and productive expert knowledge domain and then select from and transform the expert knowledge domain into a workforce continuous improvement program.

As the course mentor designs the personalized learning syllabus these are the primary questions:

- ❖ What is the skilled and productive workforce expert knowledge domain?
- ❖ What are the critical success factors associated with mentor/student dialogue?
- ❖ What is the sequence of events and schedule for the course?
- ❖ What resources and assets are needed to support the course?

An important consideration to kept in mind: companies need flexible educational opportunities that accommodate variable workforce schedules. Available online the skilled and productive personalized learning course solves the problems associated with traditional education classes, classes scheduled for place and time.

Skilled and Productive Workforce Knowledge Domain Index

Part I. Workforce and Workplace Theory

Part I. Workforce and Workplace Factors

1.0 Workforce Characteristics

Theory is the foundation of every knowledge domain. As new thoughts and new technology develop, his is the most changing aspect of knowledge domains

1.1 **DEFINITION OF WORKFORCE**. Drawing from the archives of theory and research publications, what do the terms workforce and workplace mean?

1.2 **SKILLED JOB PERFORMANCE**. Drawing from the archives of ergonomics and human factors, what does the term workforce mean?

1.3 **PRODUCTIVITY**. Drawing from the archives of management professional publications, what does the term workplace mean?

2.0 Organization Analysis

2.1 **COMPANY MANAGEMENT TRADITIONS**. What are the company management customs, norms and traditions that positively or adversely affect skilled and productive job performance?

2.2 **MANAGEMENT PROGRAM PERSPECTIVES**. To what degree do existing management program perspectives foster or impede skilled and productive job performance?

2.3 **WORK PRACTICES PROGRAM PERSPECTIVES**. To what degree do existing work practices foster or impede the development of skilled and productive job performance?

2.4 **ANTICIPATED WORK CUSTOMS.** What impact will the emphasis on skilled and productive job performance have on existing company customs regarding individual advancement?

3.0 Developing Human Resources

3.1 **EDUCATIONAL REQUIREMENTS.** What are the educational requirements associated with specific job assignments?

3.2 **DESIRED EXPERIENCE.** What are the experience requirements associated with assigned job responsibilities and activities?

3.3 **ORGANIZATION RESOURCES.** Recognizing that human resource development builds on what already exists, then to what degree do the needed workforce skills and experience exist?

3.4 **PEER ASSOCIATIONS.** What training roles can be assigned to those working with new personnel?

3.5 **INTERNSHIPS.** What internship programs should be established to help personnel more fully understand the importance of skilled and productive job performance?

3.6 **SCHOLASTIC AND HIGHER EDUCATION SUPPORT.** What training roles can be assigned to local and regional educational centers?

3.7 **RECRUITMENT AND SELECTION.** What recruitment strategies and selection standards are recommended?

3.8 **WORKFORCE ROLE IN RECRUITMENT AND SELECTION.** What role should the workforce play in recruitment and retention?

3.9 **SKILLED WORKFORCE RETENTION.** What management position and strategy is needed to assure retention of skilled personnel?

4.0 Individual Limitations and Capabilities

The following line of questioning helps us understand the importance of anticipating the limitations and capabilities of physically disabled, educationally disadvantaged, and less able workers. One item recognizes that as new products and technology become available, the possibilities for employing the disabled and disadvantaged increase. Health and human services alliances and family support are noted as critical aspects of human resource development.

4.1 **PHYSICALLY DISABLED WORKERS**. What must be done to support employees with permanent and temporary physical disabilities?

4.2 **EDUCATIONALLY DISADVANTAGED WORKERS**. How do we respond to the special expectations and requirements of educationally disadvantaged personnel?

4.3 **MENTALLY LESS ABLE WORKERS**. What innovative work environments are required for the employment of the mentally less able?

4.4 **NEW PRODUCTS AND TECHNOLOGY**. What new products and technology can increase the possibilities for employing the disabled and disadvantaged and help assure a safe, secure, and convenient environment for these workers?

4.5 **HEALTH AND HUMAN SERVICES ALLIANCES**. How can public agencies be of assistance in the design of appropriate work environments for those with job performance limitations?

Part II. Work Systems Expert Knowledge

The questions in this agenda recognize work systems are a common element in companies relying on advanced technology— service organizations rely upon computers, networks, data-storage programs, and a variety of decision support systems— company production organizations rely on manufacturing cells, computer integrated manufacturing, quality control programs, logistics and materials handling activities; all centered around work systems—activities associated with company business affairs and customer service are extensively supported by work systems.

1.0 Work System Allocations

Recognizing that production and service requirements and workflow are the bases for identifying required work systems, then:

1.1 **WORK SYSTEM REQUIREMENTS.** In support of work system activities, where are work systems required?

1.2 **WORK SYSTEM NOMENCLATURE.** What is the recommended work system nomenclature?

1.3 **ALLOCATION OF WORK SYSTEMS.** Within the work facility where should work systems be located and arranged to assure the best possible access, security, and efficient activities?

2.0 Work System-Related Activities

Each work system has its own unique combination of elements; therefore:

2.1 **PLACE IN PROCESS.** Where does the subject work system fit into the total project process?

2.2 **SPECIFIC ACTIVITIES.** What are the specific work system activities?

2.3 **OUTPUT REQUIREMENTS.** What are the specific work outputs required of the work system?

2.4 **ACTIVITIES SEQUENCE AND TIMELINE.** What task sequences and timelines characterize the activities assigned to the work system?

2.5 **COLLATERAL RESPONSIBILITIES.** Where the opportunity exists for individuals to contribute to other operations, what assignments are appropriate?

3.0 Support Requirements Specification

Perfecting of work systems begins with a specification of support requirements.

3.1 **INFORMATION SYSTEM LINKAGE.** What are the information system elements of the work system in terms of linkages to mainframes, intelligent work systems, microprocessors, terminals, displays, and input devices?

3.2 **FURNISHING REQUIREMENTS.** What are the furnishing requirements of the subject work system?

3.3 **EQUIPMENT REQUIREMENTS.** What are the equipment requirements of the subject work system?

3.4 **FIXTURE REQUIREMENTS.** What are the fixture requirements of the subject work system?

3.5 **TOOL REQUIREMENTS.** What are the tool requirements of the subject work system?

3.6 **MATERIALS REQUIREMENTS.** What are the materials requirements of the subject work system?

4.0 Work Performance Considerations.

Recognizing that the complexity of assigned tasks may exceed individual capabilities, then:

4.1 **ERROR ANTICIPATION.** What task error possibilities have been identified?

4.2 **ERROR MITIGATION.** What can be done to preclude or reduce task errors?

4.3 **RATE OF TASK LEARNING.** How quickly can assigned tasks be learned?

4.4 **JOB PERFORMANCE MEASURES.** What job performance measures should be applied?

5.0 Work Concerns.

Recognizing that assigned tasks may create difficult situations for individuals, then:

5.1 **OVERLOADING FACTORS.** What overloading possibilities have been identified?

5.2 **OVERLOADING MITIGATION.** What can be done to mitigate the effects of task overloading?

5.3 **JOB STRESS.** What possibilities for job stress have been identified?

5.4 **JOB STRESS MITIGATION.** What can be done to reduce or eliminate job stress?

5.5 **BODY POSITION.** Do work system tasks require the individual to be seated, standing, or in an awkward position for extended periods?

5.6 **BODY MOVEMENTS.** Do work system tasks require precise finger, hand, limb, hand-arm, eye/hand movements?

5.7 **BODY STRESS.** What possibilities for body stress have been identified?

5.8 **SPECIAL REQUIREMENTS.** When individuals with special limitations and requirements are assigned to the subject work system, what additional design features are required?

6.0 Operator/Automation Allocation Strategy.

Recognizing that operations may require both operator and automated task allocations, then:

6.1 **ALLOCATION CRITERIA.** What are the basic criteria for developing operator/automation allocation strategy?

6.2 **GREATER AUTOMATION.** What strategies for operator/automation allocations can be developed at the initial stages of design that will lead to greater automation?

7.0 Data Input/Output Devices.

As data input/output devices must often be incorporated into the design of work systems, then:

7.1 **INPUT DEVICES.** Where work system activities center on input display devices, what steps must be taken to assure that both hardware and software features correspond to work system tasks and activities?

7.2 **INPUT DEVICE LOCATION.** Considering task activities, work system physical features, surrounding work system characteristics, and the use of the device by other individuals, where should the input devices be located?

7.3 **DISPLAY DEVICES.** Where work system activities center around display devices, what steps must be taken to assure that both hardware and software features correspond to work system tasks and activities?

7.4 **DISPLAY LOCATION.** Considering task activities, work system physical features, surrounding work system characteristics, and the use of the display by other individuals, where should display devices be located?

8.0 Maintainability Considerations.

Recognizing that work system design must anticipate and provide for component failures, out of specification performance, and parts replacement; establish preventive measures; and offer guidelines for troubleshooting, then:

8.1 **AREAS OF CONCERN.** When designing for maintainability, what failure events are of principal concern?

8.2 **ANTICIPATED EVENTS.** What will be the effect of various work system system breakdowns?

8.3 **MAINTAINABILITY STRATEGY.** What is an effective strategy for maintaining prescribed system performance levels and restoring failed hardware and software components?

9.0 Fault Location.

Recognizing that fault location is often a complex undertaking, then:

9.1 **TROUBLESHOOTING GUIDELINES**. What troubleshooting guidelines can be of assistance to personnel?

9.2 **TROUBLESHOOTING GUIDELINES EVALUATION**. Are procedures easily understood and as free of ambiguity as possible?

9.3 **WORK SYSTEM FAILURE DOCUMENTATION**. What documentation best provides for the retention of circumstances surrounding failure and crisis events?

10.0 Review of Recommendations.

Recognizing that work system design recommendations require assessment from the perspective of skilled job performance, then:

10.1 **PROPOSED WORK SYSTEM FEATURES**. Considering that work systems have unique activities and support requirements, what are the proposed work system features?

10.2 **DESIGN CRITIQUE**. Which work system design proposals most effectively meet the organization's concern for attaining and maintaining skilled job performance?

10.3 **ASSIGNED PERSONNEL CRITIQUE**. Which design recommendations most effectively meet the expectations and requirements expressed by assigned personnel?

10.4 **RECOMMENDATION IMPACT**. Which proposals would require substantial accommodation on the part of organizations and assigned personnel?

10.5 **ATTAINING AGREEMENT**. Which recommendations are likely to be unsuccessful unless organization and individual viewpoints are changed?

Part III. ICT Expert Knowledge

Information and communication technology (ICT) development are features of work system design. The following questions items identify information development and processing tasks that are of special importance, complex or unique, or subject to information overload. Concerns identified include: ease of use, reduction of operational complexity, limiting the number of software products, providing for rapid changeover to new applications, and minimizing disruption caused by new software releases. Opportunities for application of database support, decision-making aids, and expert and knowledge system support are identified through question applications.

1.0 Information and Communication Technology Systems Tasks.

ICT systems are elemental units of work system design; therefore:

1.1 **SPECIFIC INFORMATION AND COMMUNICATION ACTIVITIES**. What are the specific ICT monitoring, development, exchange, and application responsibilities assigned to this work system?

1.2 **ROLE IN TOTAL INFORMATION AND COMMUNICATION SYSTEM**. In what way will the communications and information developed at this work system be used within the total facility operations?

1.3 **INFORMATION AND COMMUNICATION SOURCES**. What elements within the total facility system provide information to and communicate with the work system?

1.4 **INFORMATION AND COMMUNICATION DESTINATIONS**. What elements within the total facility system receive information and communications from the work system?

1.5 **IMPORTANT CONTACTS**. Which individuals and groups provide information and communications of special importance to this work system?

1.6 **WORK SYSTEM INTERFACE**. What procedures, activities, and equipment connect the information and communication system to the total work system?

1.7 **INFORMAL CONTACTS**. What individuals and groups are informal sources of information?

2.0 Complex or Unique Tasks.

It is important to identify information and communication system development and processing tasks that are complex or unique, therefore:

2.1 **TASK COMPLEXITY**. What is the relative complexity or uniqueness of the identified information and communication development and processing activities?

2.2 **INFORMATION OVERLOAD**. As information overload is often a concern, what sequencing, task simplification, and feedback features should be incorporated into work system information and communication system design?

2.3 **AUTOMATED SYSTEM ELEMENTS**. As it is important to automate information and communication development tasks wherever possible, what tasks are candidates for automation?

2.4 **PERFORMANCE EVALUATIONS**. What information and communication system performance evaluations will help confirm the features of the proposed system?

3.0 Essential Applications Features.

This is another source of insight as to what is important to the work system design. Therefore, you might pursue the following:

3.1 **WORK SYSTEM APPLICATIONS**. What specific work system

information and communication system activities require applications support?

3.2 **DATA AND INFORMATION TYPES.** What information and data types pertain to the work system?

3.3 **EXTENT OF USE.** How many different work systems will employ the prospective applications?

3.4 **USER INTERFACE ENHANCEMENT.** Application design must anticipate the information and communication system operator's manner of thought and behavior; therefore: What is required of the application in terms of supporting text, graphic, and audio inputs and outputs?

3.5 **AREAS OF CONCERN.** Where will it be particularly important to assure that information and communication system technology is designed for ease of use?

3.6 **NEW RELEASES DISRUPTION.** When new application releases are introduced, what safeguards will be developed to preclude disruption of information and communication system operations and content?

Part IV. Work System Development Risk Analysis

1.0 Assessing Work System Design Proposals

The objective here is to provide the means for the workforce to develop work system design proposals that require assessment from the perspective of skilled job performance, then:

1.1 **PROPOSED WORK SYSTEM DESIGN CRITIQUE.** Which work system design proposals most effectively meet the organization's concern for attaining and maintaining skilled job performance?

1.2 **ASSIGNED PERSONNEL CRITIQUE.** Which work system design recommendations most effectively meet the expectations and requirements expressed by assigned personnel?

1.3 **RECOMMENDATION IMPACT.** Which work system design proposals require substantial accommodation on the part of the organization and assigned personnel?

1.4 **ATTAINING AGREEMENT.** Which program proposals are likely to be unsuccessful unless organization and individual viewpoints are changed?

2.0 Business Plan

2.1 **BUSINESS PLAN.** What business plan is proposed to respond to work system development financial constraints, anticipated pitfalls, and ethical considerations?

2.2 **FINANCIAL REQUIREMENTS.** What are the financial requirements for the various development phases of the work system development project?

2.3 **OPERATING COSTS.** What are the anticipated operating costs for the work system, prior to start, during first period of operation, and over time?

2.4 **OVERSIGHT.** What is the oversight process for milestone approvals and scheduled allocation of funds for each phase of the work system development project?

2.5 **FUNDING SOURCES.** What are the possible funding sources for the development project?

2.6 **COMPETITIVE FUNDING REQUEST.** What steps must be taken to make the request for funding as competitive and attractive as possible?

2.7 **COMMUNITY BENEFITS.** As the work system development project means jobs and increased economic activity in the local community, what is the best way to present these benefits?

2.8 **CONSEQUENCES FOR LIMITED OR NON-FUNDING FOR THE PROPOSED WORK SYSTEM DEVELOPMENT.** What are the consequences to the company if the proposed work system is not funded or limited?

Part V. Learn-by-Doing: Develop a Continuous Improvement Program

Following the study of expert knowledge, individuals and groups are encouraged to establish a work system continuous improvement program.

1.0 Work Group Continuous Improvement Program

Encompassing the entire scope of the acquired skilled job performance and work system expert knowledge, the following question items suggest initial deliberations for workforce groups establishing a continuous improvement program:

1.1 **CONTINUOUS IMPROVEMENT PROGRAM OBJECTIVES**. What are the continuous improvement program objectives?

1.2 **PROGRAM CRITICAL ISSUES**. What are the critical issues associated with the continuous improvement program?

1.3 **PROGRAM DEVELOPMENT ACTION PLAN**. What are the research and development activities needed to develop the continuous improvement program?

1.4 **PROGRAM DEVELOPMENT TIMELINE**. What is the sequence of events and schedule for the continuous improvement program?

1.5 **NEEDED RESOURCES AND ASSETS**. What resources and assets are needed to support the program action plan?

1.6 **INFORMATION SECURITY MANDATES**. In terms of protecting proprietary interests what are the program information security mandates?

2.0 Management and Workforce Perspectives

The continuous improvement program is developed in

collaboration with company managers and workforce colleagues, therefore:

2.1 **MANAGEMENT PERSPECTIVES**. What are the company's managers concerns and expectations for the proposed continuous improvement program?

2.2 **WORKFORCE PERSPECTIVES**. What are the workforce's concerns and expectations for the proposed continuous improvement program?

2.3 **EXISTING TRAINING PROGRAMS**. What company training programs can provide information and expertise that pertain to the proposed continuous improvement program?

3.0 Changing Conditions

The continuous improvement program must be responsive to changing conditions within company organizations, therefore:

3.1 **REDIRECTION OF PROGRAM OBJECTIVES**. What situations or events might lead to the modification or redirection of continuous improvement program objectives?

3.2 **CHANGING RESPONSIBILITIES AND ACTIVITIES**. Considering the possibilities for corporate redesign, restructuring, and redefinition, where are organization responsibilities and activities likely to change?

3.3 **NEW TECHNOLOGY**. Where and to what extent is new technology incorporated into the company's existing work system?

3.4 **PROGRAM REQUIRED SKILLS**. What are the skill requirements associated with continuous improvement program responsibilities and assigned activities?

Study 4. A Knowledge Sharing Research Strategy, Directed to Changing Social and Economic Conditions

In this study you will recognize a traditional teaching strategy—to show students how much they have learned take them on to something new.

The topic selected to confirm the value of knowledge sharing theory, method, and process is an area of family and community life stressed by changing social and economic conditions: the frail elderly living at home and their caregivers.

Across the globe from Japan, China, and Australia to Europe, America, and Canada we see with the increase in elderly populations and changing social and economies a breaking up traditional family life, changing the quality of life for the frail elderly. Once family and friends were in daily contact with the frail elderly, now we see as a result of social and economic circumstance the frail elderly living without direct family and friend support; a role now being fulfilled by professional home caregivers with many types of responsibilities.

Of course, putting social and economics circumstance aside, we will always find the frail elderly wanting to live at home, saying: "I'll move only if I have to. I want to stay at home, stay with my family life memories and old friends, and have the comfort of being in my old neighborhood."

Note, we use the term "frail elderly." However, we maintain the awareness that this label may evoke an unfortunate image. When you use this term you must discard stereotypes and perceive the frail elderly to be in personal, social, and economic evolution. You must be alert to the fact that the home life of the frail elderly is becoming more complex and their need for perfected home settings and services more pressing.

A Business Enterprise

The promise of the expanding frail elderly home care market has brought promising possibilities for a business enterprise. However, size of market does not necessarily assure success. This business enterprise requires critical thinking and thorough analysis to define opportunity and develop promising quality of life innovations. In particular, the need to discover the extent and variety of home care requirements

Expert Knowledge

The promise and needs of the expanding frail elderly and caregiver customer base has brought information and communication technology (ICT) systems and service innovations to mind. For business enterprise success, you must recognize that the frail elderly are too diverse a population to be considered in simple terms. For this, the knowledge sharing research strategy has these beginning points: gaining insights into the frail elderly and caregivers' expectations and requirements and interpretation of these insights as they apply to the design and development of ICT–based systems and services.

The expert knowledge you develop is directed to critical considerations, such as the following provided by the *Australian Government Department of Health and Ageing*, showing that quality of life for the frail elderly living at home includes a number of considerations, directed to homecare services challenges and nursing care responsibilities, such as:

- ❖ Establish a flexible, convenient, and affordable homecare ICT solution.
- ❖ Establish an Aged Care Assessment Team to conduct needs analysis.
- ❖ Help older people to remain in their own home for as long as possible.
- ❖ Help ensue people get the right level of care.
- ❖ Help ensure that the fees people pay are fair.
- ❖ Establish a information resources, consultations, and referral services.

Homecare Challenges

These always require detailed analysis, such as:

- ❖ The preferred level of daily and social independence.
- ❖ Access to information about the care options available and the facts.
- ❖ Access to the details of the care being provided, such as assistance with oxygen apparatus and internal feeding.
- ❖ Developing a package of care that best meets individual needs.

Home Nursing Care Responsibilities

Consider the details of this range of home quality of life considerations for the frail elderly:

- ❖ Care by health professionals such as a physiotherapist, podiatrist, and other types of allied health care.
- ❖ Personal care.
- ❖ Transportation to appointments.
- ❖ Social support.

- ❖ Meals and other food services.
- ❖ Home cleaning services.
- ❖ Emergency response capabilities.

Business Enterprise Participants

In addition to business enterprise staff participation the following should be knowledge sharing research participants:

- ❖ The frail elderly and families and friends who have insightful understanding about the best way to meet home life, health care, and service expectations and requirements.
- ❖ Professional healthcare and service providers who know all about maintaining quality of life for the frail elderly ageing in place.
- ❖ Communities of interest such as families and neighborhood groups, regulatory entities, social service consultants, and gerontologists, who have special interests and knowledge.

Critique of Findings

A final thought regarding knowledge sharing strategic research. At no time do we set aside a sense of critique, keeping questions such as these in mind:

- ❖ What frail elderly activities were overlooked within the study of individual differences, daily activities, areas of concern, and in-home healthcare?
- ❖ Within the record of deliberations are their misleading or incomplete statements?
- ❖ What alternative interpretations of findings within the record of deliberations would you like to suggest?
- ❖ Have all unresolved issues been identified?

Business Enterprise Deliberation Agenda

Part I. Concept Development and Evaluation

1.0 The Enterprise Vision

1.1 **ENTERPRISE VISION**. Advances in technology and the need to provide for the quality of life experience of the frail elderly at home have produced an unlimited opportunity, therefore: what is the enterprise vision?

1.2 **ENTERPRISE OUTCOME**. Characterized by strong quality of life-orientation, the benefits of technology on the wellbeing and life style of the frail elderly ageing at home, and a cost-effective solution, what is the anticipated enterprise outcome?

2.0 Pathway to Innovation

2.1 **LIMITATIONS AND CAPABILITIES OF THE FRAIL ELDERLY**. Where has the work of gerontologists, psychophysiologists, and health care professionals achieved new understanding of the limitations and capabilities of the frail elderly?

2.2 **ADVANCES IN TECHNOLOGY**. What advances in information and communication technology (ICT) have the potential to significantly improve the quality of life of the frail elderly living at home?

2.3 **HOME DESIGN INNOVATIONS**. Where are fundamental changes in housing remodeling and retirement communities for the frail elderly taking place?

2.4 **COMPETING CONCEPTS**. What corporations and businesses are providing quality of life systems to the frail elderly and what are the features of their product lines and price?

Part II. The Frail Elderly at Home

3.0 Individual Differences

3.1 **DISTINGUISHING CHARACTERISTICS**. What characteristics and factors can be used to distinguish the frail elderly who wish to continue to live at home as they age?

3.2 **SELF PERCEPTIONS**. How do the frail elderly perceive themselves, family members, and care givers in terms of their individual privacy rights and sense of independence?

3.3 **SOCIAL LIFE**. What are the social customs, relationship norms, and cultural traditions of the frail elderly?

3.4 **RECREATION AND LEISURE PREFERENCES**. What are the recreation and leisure interests of the frail elderly?

3.5 **CONTINUITY WITH THE PAST**. In what ways are the frail elderly sensitive to suggestions for changing the features of their home?

4.0 Daily Activities

4.1 **COMMON HOME ACTIVITIES**. What are the daily activities characteristic of common home spaces: parking, entryway, living room, bedroom, kitchen, bath, home office?

4.2 **ACTIVITY LEVELS**. What is known about the extent, time of occurrence, and duration of daily activities in the home?

4.3 **SENSE OF INDEPENDENT LIVING**. Where do we find the frail elderly most demanding when protecting their sense of independence?

4.4 **MAINTAIN HOUSEKEEPING STANDARDS**. Such as the instance of maintaining cleanliness and order, where do we find common housekeeping tasks difficult to undertake?

4.5 **MEAL PREPARATION**. Where is it difficult for the frail elderly to prepare meals and maintain their cuisine and diet preferences?

4.6 **PERSONAL HEALTHCARE.** What health care régimes and medication schedules are most challenging for the frail elderly?

4.7 **FAMILY AND FRIEND CARE PROVIDERS.** How do family and friend care providers go about meeting the expectations and requirements of the frail elderly?

4.8 **IN-HOME HEALTH CARE SERVICES.** How do inn-home health care providers go about meeting the expectations and requirements of the frail elderly?

5.0 Areas of Concern

5.1 **COGNITIVE ABILITIES.** what activities requiring cognitive abilities are challenging for the frail elderly?

5.2 **PERCEPTUAL AND MOTOR SKILLS.** what activities requiring perceptual and motor skills are challenging for the frail elderly?

5.3 **INDIVIDUAL MOBILITY.** What mobility limitations and the use of walking aids and wheelchairs, daily and in emergencies, considerations are essential to recognize during ICT system design deliberations?

5.4 **ACCIDENT PREVENTION.** The frail elderly can have accidents anywhere in the home; therefore, in this case, what is essential to consider during ICT system design deliberations?

5.5 **EDUCATIONALLY DISADVANTAGED.** What must be considered during ICT system design deliberations regarding the special expectations and requirements of educationally disadvantaged personnel, i.e. can't read, unfamiliar with computers, and dislike of appliances in general?

5.6 **MENTALLY AND EMOTIONALLY LESS ABLE.** What must be considered during ICT system design deliberations in terms of accommodating the mentally and emotionally less able?

6.0 In-Home Heath Care

6.1 **PERSONAL HEALTH CARE**. Health care régimes and medication schedules can challenge the frail elderly, therefore, how can the ICT system serve as an aid?

6.2 **PHYSICALLY DISABLED**. What must be considered when accommodating ICT systems to the requirements of the frail elderly ageing at home with permanent and temporary physical disabilities?

6.3 **PERIODS OF RECOVERY**. How can ICT system features be used to aid the frail elderly when recovering from an illness or hospital treatment?

6.4 **HEALTH CARE PROFESSIONALS**. What home ICT features are required for the activities of health care professionals?

6.5 **HEALTH CARE DESIGN CHALLENGES**. In summary, what are the ICT system requirements associated with health care in-home services?

Part III. The Information and Communication System

7.0 ICT System Design Proposals

7.1 **A PROPOSED DESIGN CONCEPT**. Characterized by its benefits on the wellbeing and lifestyle of older people ageing at home every participant in the standard of performance application may propose a design concept, therefore: what is the proposed design concept and to which spaces, entry way, living room, bedroom, kitchen, bath, home office, does it apply?

7.2 **DESIGN CONCEPT EVALUATION**. Does the design concept proposal offer well-thought-out and well-researched alternate proposals, alternate viewpoints, and dissenting opinions?

7.3 **INFORMATIVE PROPOSAL.** Is the design proposal supported by noteworthy research references?

7.4 **PROBLEM ANTICIPATION.** Does the design concept identify and offer plausible solutions to problems or issues?

7.5 **NEW ICT PRODUCTS AND TECHNOLOGY.** What new ICT products and technology are needed to fulfill the promise of the proposed design concept?

7.6. **ADDITIONAL RESEARCH.** What additional research is needed to confirm the design concept proposal?

7.7 **CONTINUAL EVALUATION.** Once the design concept is established what evaluation program should be put in place to assess progress and identify possibilities for concept improvement?

8.0 Health Care Considerations

8.1 **SUPPORTING HEALTH CARE ACTIVITIES.** Considering the expectations and requirements for establishing a therapeutic environment for the frail elderly at home: how can ICT systems be designed to more effectively support home care activities?

8.2 **THERAPEUTIC ENVIRONMENTS.** What ICT system features will help establish a therapeutic environment for the frail elderly at home?

8.3 **HEALTH CARE ACTIVITY SUPPORT.** Considering the care and treatment provided in the home to the frail elderly, what ICT furnishing, fixtures, and equipment options, fixed or mobile, do home spaces require?

8.4 **EMERGENCY ICT.** In terms of individual safety and emergency events, what special ICT measures are necessary?

9.0 Integrated ICT Systems

9.1 **INTEGRATED SYSTEM REQUIREMENTS.** In terms of quality of life, therapeutic possibilities, and care and treatment requirements, what ICT system automated, programmed, and manual controls are needed?

9.2 **MONITORING SYSTEMS**. To automate the ICT system, what are activity and ambient environment monitoring systems are required?

9.3 **GRAPHIC USER INTERFACE ENHANCEMENT**. Anticipating the frail elders' manner of thought and behavior; where will it be particularly important to assure that the system graphic user interface is designed for ease of use; in terms of supporting text, graphics, and audio inputs and outputs?

9.4 **LIMITING THE NUMBER OF UNIQUE FEATURES**. The frail elderly are best served by limiting the number and unique features of system controls, therefore: what system characteristics meet these criteria?

9.5 **DECISION SUPPORT FEATURES**. Successful ICT integrated systems require knowledge support; therefore: what opportunities exist for application of database, decision support, and expert and knowledge system support within the ICT system?

9.6 **NEW RELEASES DISRUPTION**. When new software releases are introduced, what instructional safeguards will be developed to preclude disruption of ICT system operations?

9.7 **EASE OF USE**. Where will it be particularly important to assure that ICT system control features are designed for ease of use?

9.8 **ICT SYSTEM FIXTURE FEATURES**. What are the fixture requirements for integrated ICT system components?

10.0 ICT System Installation

10.1 **REMODELING THE HOME**. To what extent will a home have to be remodeled to accommodate the integrated ICT system?

10.2 **NEW HOME DESIGN**. The integrated ICT system can be a significant feature for both new housing developments and retirement communities; so, what is the best way to package all of the system information to guide interior architectural design?

10.3 **INSTALLATION ALTERNATIVES AND OPTIONS**. What are the installation alternatives and options for proposed ICT systems?

10.4 **AUTOMATED BUILDING SYSTEMS COMPATIBILITY**. Where do opportunities exist for integrating ICT systems into automated building systems?

10.5 **COSTS TO BUYERS**. What are the costs to buyer estimates for the components of the proposed ICT system?

10.6 **INSTALLATION COSTS**. What are the anticipated installation costs for the proposed ICT system?

10.7 **ENERGY CONSERVATION**. How can ICT systems features be used to conserve energy?

10.8 **MAINTAINABILITY CONSIDERATIONS**. Recognizing that ICT system design must anticipate and provide for component failures, out of specification performance, and parts replacement; establish preventive measures; and offer guidelines for troubleshooting, then: What is an effective strategy for maintaining prescribed system performance levels and restoring failed hardware and software components?

10.9 **ICT SYSTEM MANUAL AND INSTRUCTIONAL VIDEO**. This is a very important requirement. The manual and instructional video must be more than how to operate the system; it must inform and encourage use, therefore: What should be included in the ICT system presentations so the frail elderly understand fully all the system benefits, uses, and how to effectively operate the system?

Part III. Learn-by-Doing Assignments

From the perspective that writing is an intense learning experience, in the tutorial knowledge sharing assignments participants, individually and in groups, address a learning resource promising opportunity, challenging problem, or changing condition of interest:

1. Sign Into the Tutorial Web Site

2. Define the Evolving Learning Resource Study Objectives and Critical Success Factors

3. Develop Annotated Expert Knowledge References

4. Develop the Project Deliberation Agenda

5. Share Assignment Outcomes with Colleagues for Critique

Use Lesson 3: Section 3.1 Managing the Knowledge Sharing Process as a guideline for developing your study objectives. When managing a project-specific knowledge sharing process, this deliberation agenda guides the development project critical success factors and scope of work ranging from defining the learning resource project objectives to building the knowledge sharing deliberation agenda to your means for evaluating findings and outcomes.

To provide for evaluation of their work, participants place each completed phase of the assignment in the tutorial Web site for the assignment mentor's and tutorial participants' critique.